NATIONAL GEOGRAPHIC

School Publishing

Then and Now

Jenny Lee

PICTURE CREDITS
Cover, 15 (below), North Wind Picture Archives; Cover (inset), 1 (below), 2, 4 (above), 4 (below), 5 (left), 6, 7 (left), 7 (above), 8 (below), 9 (right below), 10 (left), 12 (below), 14 (left), 14 (right), 16 (left), 17 (above), 18 (left), 19 (above), APL/Corbis; 1 (above), 8 (above), 9 (left below), 9 (right above), 10 (right), 11 (right), 12 (above), 16 (right), 18 (right below), Photolibrary.com; 5 (right), 11 (left), 15 (above), 17 (below), 18 (right above), Getty Images; 9 (above left), Mary Evans Picture Library; 13 (above), isifa Image Service s.r.o./Alamy; 13 (below), David Martyn Hughes/Alamy; 19 (below), Jeff Greenberg/PhotoEdit.

Produced through the worldwide resources of the National Geographic Society, John M. Fahey, Jr., President and Chief Executive Officer; Gilbert M. Grosvenor, Chairman of the Board; Nina D. Hoffman, Executive Vice President and President, Books and Education Publishing Group.

PREPARED BY NATIONAL GEOGRAPHIC SCHOOL PUBLISHING
Steve Mico, Executive Vice President and Publisher, Children's Books and Education Publishing Group; Marianne Hiland, Editor in Chief; Lynnette Brent, Executive Editor; Michael Murphy and Barbara Wood, Senior Editors; Nicole Rouse, Editor; Bea Jackson, Design Director; David Dumo, Art Director; Shanin Glenn, Designer; Margaret Sidlosky, Illustrations Director; Matt Wascavage, Manager of Publishing Services; Sean Philpotts, Production Manager.

MANUFACTURING AND QUALITY MANAGEMENT
Christopher A. Liedel, Chief Financial Officer; Phillip L. Schlosser, Vice President; Clifton M. Brown III, Director.

BOOK DEVELOPMENT
Ibis for Kids Australia Pty Limited.

Published by the National Geographic Society
1145 17th Street, N.W.
Washington, D.C. 20036-4688

Product No. 4W1005053

ISBN-13: 978-1-4263-5049-8
ISBN-10: 1-4263-5049-X

2010 2009 2008
4 5 6 7 8 9 10 11 12 13 14 15

Printed in China

Contents

Think and Discuss	4
Looking Back at the Past	6
Machines	8
Communication	10
Transportation	12
Cities	14
Learning	16
Use What You Learned	18
Picture Glossary	20

Think and Discuss

What was it like to live 100 years ago? How have people's lives changed since then?

watching television

cars and trucks

Looking Back at the Past

Have you ever seen photos of people from **long ago**? Old photos can help us learn about **the past**.

This old photograph shows a family ready to go bike riding.

This photograph shows one of the first cars.

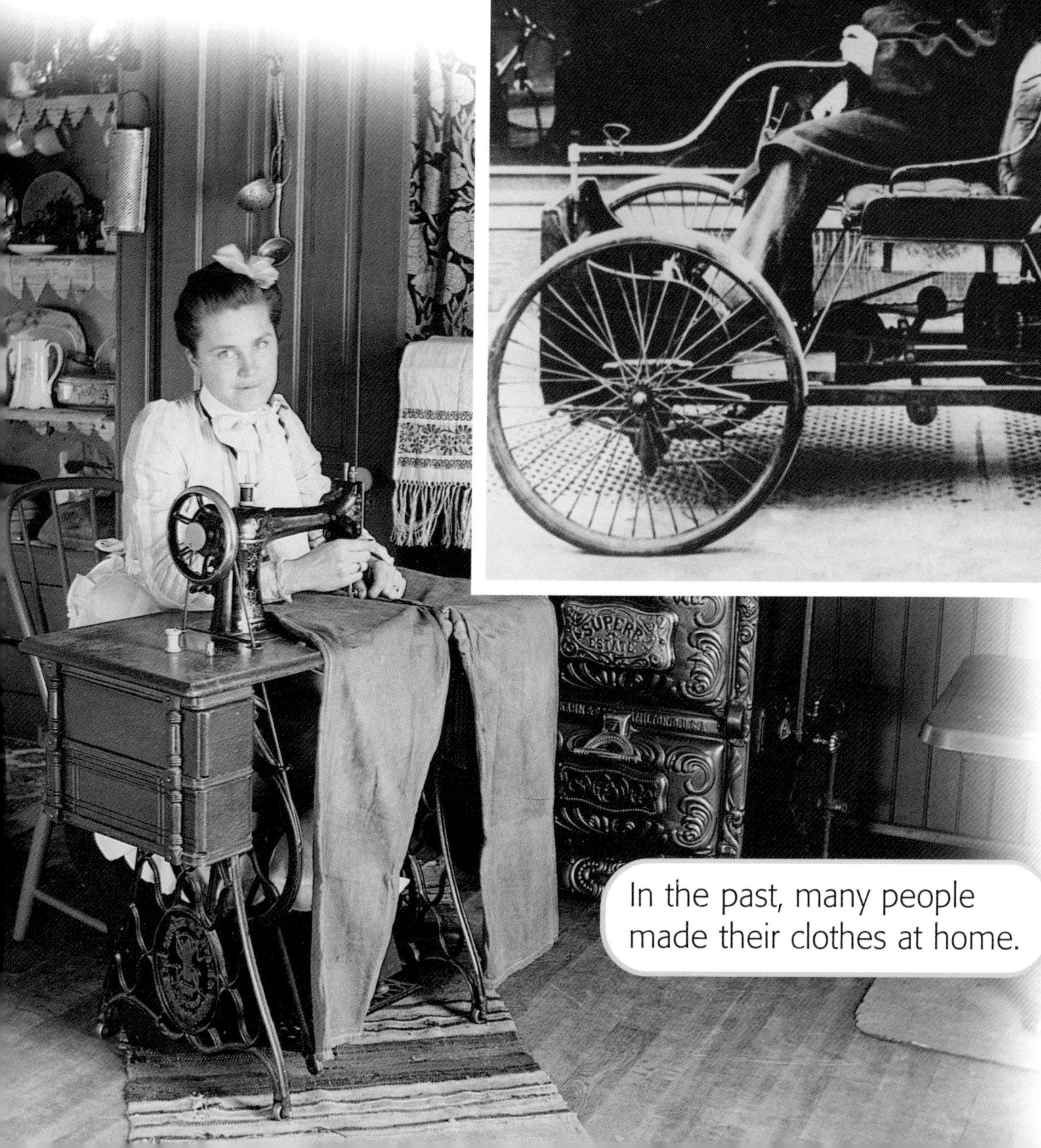

In the past, many people made their clothes at home.

Machines

Today people use many different **machines** at home. What did people use in the past?

Before there were washing machines, people washed their clothes by hand.

Before there were refrigerators, people used ice boxes to keep food cool.

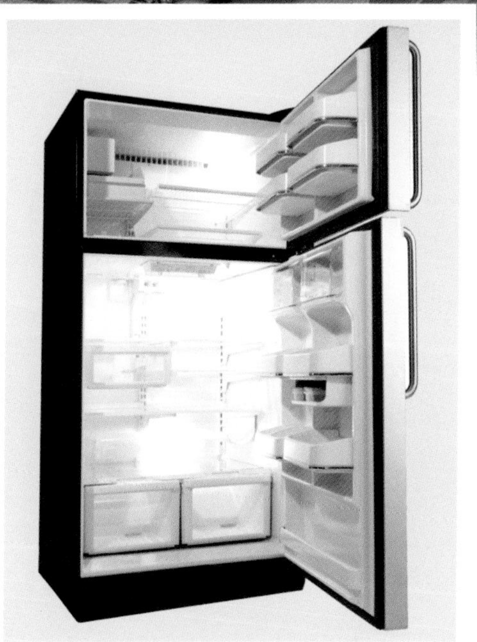

Before there were electric and gas stoves, people used wood-burning stoves.

Communication

Today we have many ways to communicate. How did people communicate in the past?

Computers and e-mail have **changed** the way people communicate.

Long ago, people used quill pens and ink to write letters.

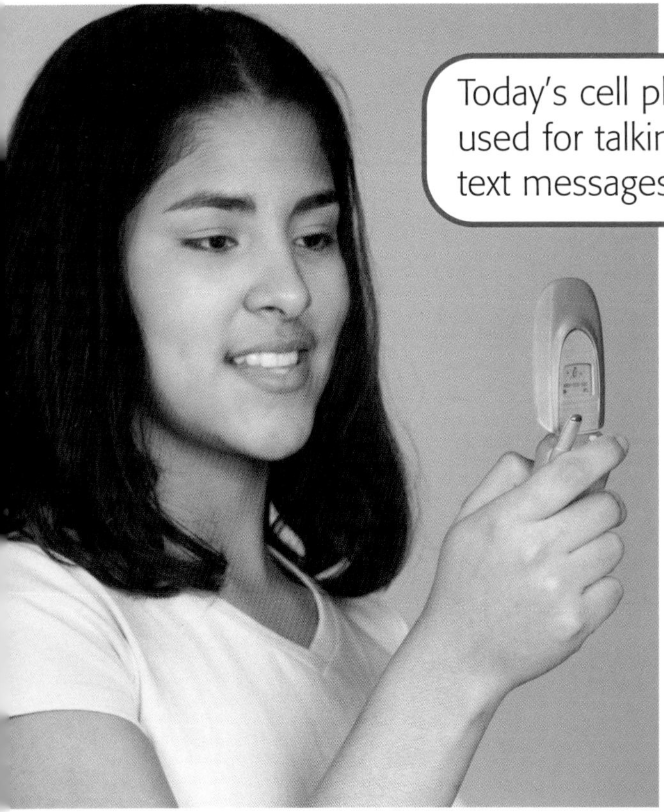

Today's cell phones can be used for talking and for sending text messages and pictures.

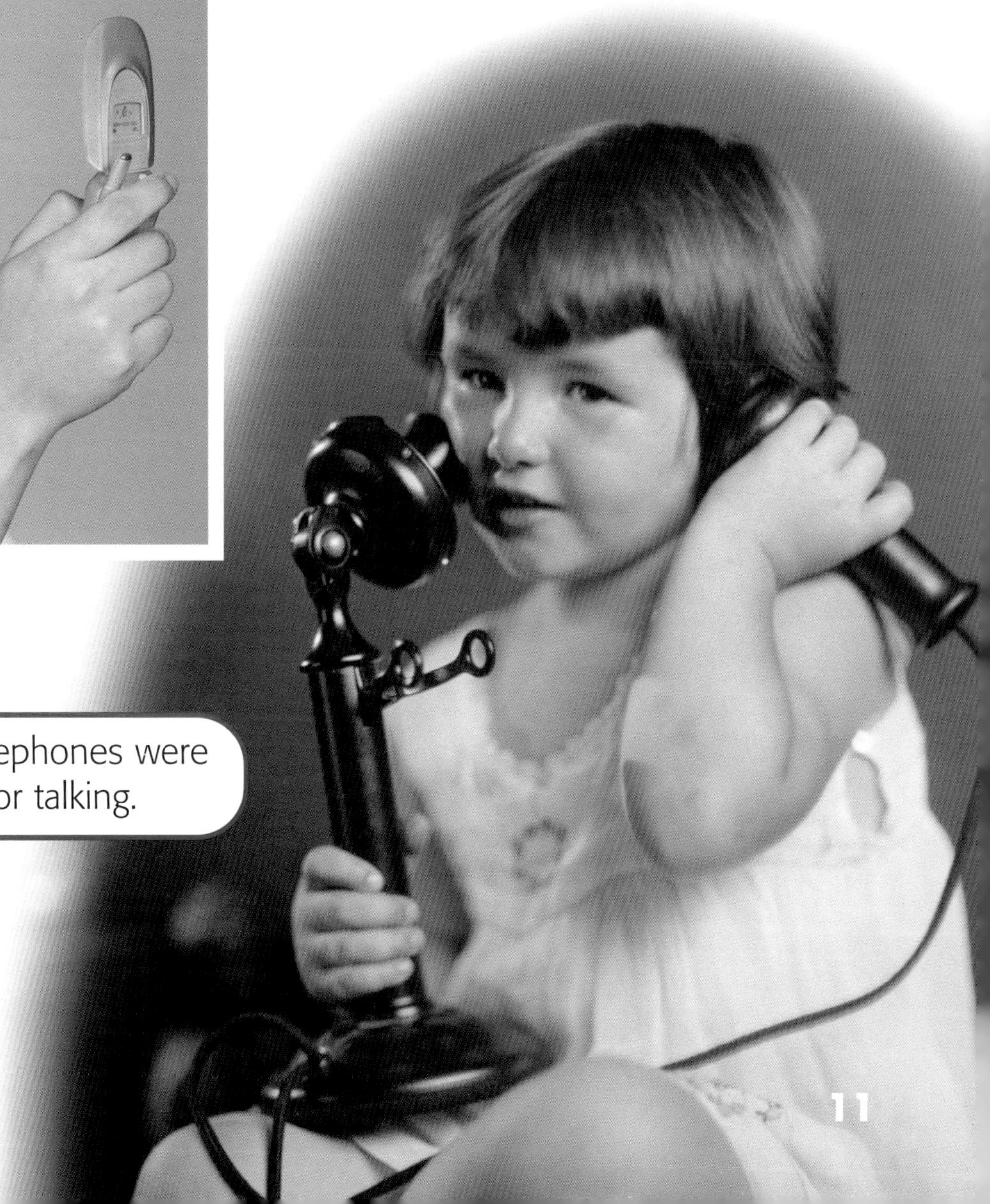

The first telephones were used only for talking.

Transportation

Today people use many different kinds of transportation. What kinds of transportation did people use in the past?

Before cars were **invented**, people used horses and buggies to travel around.

Before there were electric trains, there were steam-powered trains.

Cities

Today most cities have many tall buildings and many roads and highways. What were cities like in the past?

Boston, Massachusetts, 1870s

Modern-day Chicago, Illinois

Modern-day Hong Kong

New York City, 1900s

Learning

Today people learn about the world in many different ways. How did people learn about the world in the past?

In the past, people used books to get information. Now people also use computers, at **school** and at home.

Before there was television, people listened to the radio.

Use What You Learned

How are these people learning about the past? How can you learn about the past?

change

invent

long ago

machine

school

the past

Picture Glossary

car

cell phone

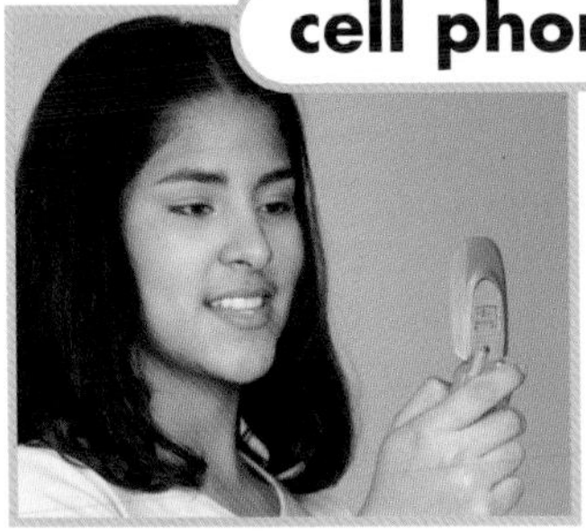

computer

horse and buggy

long ago

school